Macramé Knots Bible

The Ultimate Beginner's Guide to Handmade Braids with Step-by-Step Design Tutorials and 160 Colorful Photos

Weave Wonders

Table of content

Introduction 5

Chapter 1 7

The Art of Macramé 7

A Brief History 8

    Materials and Tools You'll Need 8

    Understanding Macramé Terms 10

    Choosing the Right Cord and Supplies 11

Setting Up Your Workspace 12

    Set Up a Comfortable Work Surface 13

    Consider Ergonomics and Comfort 14

Why is Macrame so Popular 15

Chapter 2 17

Basic Macrame Knots for Beginners 17

    Lark's Head Knot 17

    Cow Hitch Knot (Reverse Lark's Head Knot) 19

    Square Knot 20

    Double Half Hitch Knot 24

DIY Macrame Bag with Comfy Braided Handles 26

    DIY Macramé Bag..27

Macrame Hat Hanger Pattern 43

Boho Macrame Wall Hanging with Tassels 61

Dollar Tree DIY Mini Macrame Wall Hangings 79

Wall Hanging) Plant Hanger...91

....101

Crescent Moon DIY Macramé Dream Catcher....................................102

Troubleshooting and Tips 117

Common Mistakes and How to Avoid Them 117

Tips for Perfect Tension 118

Finishing Techniques..119

Conclusion 120

The Joy of Creating with Macramé 120

Continuing Your Macramé Journey 120

PREFACE

In a fast-paced world dominated by technology, the ancient art of macramé offers a serene escape, inviting us to slow down and engage in mindful creativity. This book is born from a passion for knotting and a desire to share the joy and satisfaction of creating with one's hands.

Macramé is more than just tying knots; it is a meditative practice that connects us to a rich history of craftsmanship. From intricate wall hangings to delicate jewelry, macramé has captivated generations with its versatility and elegance. Whether you are a complete beginner or an experienced artist looking to expand your repertoire, this book is designed to be your companion in exploring the endless possibilities of macramé.

On these pages, you will find a carefully curated collection of projects that range from simple to complex, each accompanied by detailed instructions and step-by-step photographs. Our goal is to inspire you to experiment, create, and discover the satisfaction of transforming simple materials into works of art.

Embark on this journey with an open heart and a willingness to explore. May the art of macramé bring you peace, joy, and a renewed appreciation for the beauty of handmade crafts.

HAPPY KNOTTING!

INTRODUCTION

My grandmother would sit in a small sunlit room, surrounded by colorful threads and the soft hum of creativity, her fingers deftly weaving intricate patterns. As a child, I watched in awe as she transformed simple strands into beautiful tapestries, each knot telling a story. This was my first introduction to the macramé world, where art and craft intertwine to create something truly magical.

Macramé is more than just a craft; it is a journey of self-expression and mindfulness. Originating centuries ago, this art form has traveled through cultures and generations, evolving yet remaining timeless. From the elegant fringes of a wall hanging to the delicate loops of a bracelet, each piece carries the essence of those who have come before us.

For many, macramé is a therapeutic escape from the hustle and bustle of daily life. The rhythmic repetition of knots becomes a form of meditation, a way to connect with oneself while creating something tangible and beautiful. As you embark on this journey, you'll discover the joy of making with your hands and the satisfaction of seeing your vision take shape.

This book is your guide to exploring the art of macramé. Whether you are a beginner eager to learn the basics or an experienced crafter looking to deepen your skills, you'll find many inspiring projects and techniques. Each chapter is crafted to build your confidence and ignite your creativity, with step-by-step instructions and tips to ensure success.

Join me as we delve into the enchanting world of macramé. Together, we will create pieces that are not only beautiful but meaningful, woven with stories of patience, passion, and perseverance. Let the threads of macramé connect us to a rich tradition of artistry and craftsmanship, and may this journey bring you as much joy and fulfillment as it has brought me.

CHAPTER 1

THE ART OF MACRAMÉ

Macramé is a technique that involves creating patterns by tying knots in string, cord, or rope. Unlike weaving or knitting, which require tools like needles or looms, macramé relies solely on the skill of the hands, making it accessible to anyone willing to learn.

The tactile nature of this craft allows for a unique connection between the creator and the material, resulting in pieces that are as much about the journey as they are about the finished product.

A Brief History

The origins of macramé date back to the 13th century, when Arabic weavers used decorative knots to finish the edges of woven textiles, a technique known as "migramah," meaning fringe. The craft spread to Europe through the Moors in Spain and became a popular pastime among sailors during long voyages, who used macramé to pass the time and create items for trade at ports.

By the Renaissance, macramé had reached England, where Queen Mary II popularized the craft at court. It experienced a significant revival during the Victorian era, when it became a favored domestic activity, allowing women to create elaborate decorations for their homes. The 1960s and 70s saw another resurgence, with the craft becoming a symbol of the counterculture movement, embodying ideals of anti-industrialism and personal expression.

Today, macramé enjoys renewed popularity as an art form and a therapeutic hobby. Modern macramé artists blend traditional techniques with contemporary aesthetics, creating everything from wall hangings to fashion accessories.

Materials and Tools You'll Need

To begin your macramé journey, you'll need some basic materials and tools:

- Cords: The foundation of any macramé project, cords come in various materials such as cotton, hemp, and jute. For beginners, a 4-6 mm cotton cord is ideal for most projects, offering a balance of strength and flexibility

- Scissors: A sharp pair of scissors is essential for clean cuts and precise trimming of cords
- Measuring Tools: A tape measure or ruler is crucial for ensuring accurate cord lengths and symmetry in your designs
- Support Tools: Depending on your project, you might need a dowel, wooden ring, or a macramé board to hold your work in place. S-hooks and corkboards can also provide stability as you work

Optional Tools: While not essential, a tapestry needle can help finish touches, and a macramé board with notches can aid in maintaining tension and pattern consistency

Armed with these materials and tools, you are ready to explore the creative possibilities of macramé, transforming simple cords into intricate designs and beautiful creations.

Understanding Macramé Terms

Before diving into projects, familiarize yourself with some fundamental macramé terminology. Knowing these terms will make it easier to follow patterns and instructions:

- Cord: The primary material used in macramé, available in various materials and thicknesses.
- Knot: The basic unit of macramé, created by intertwining cords. Common knots include the square knot, lark's head knot, and half hitch.
- Working Cord: The cord(s) that you actively use to create knots.

- Filler Cord: The stationary cord(s) around which knots are tied.
- Bight: The loop formed by folding a cord back on itself.
- Sennit: A sequence of knots tied in a continuous pattern.
- Fringe: The loose ends of cords left at the bottom of a project for decorative purposes.
- Mounting: Attaching cords to a dowel or other support structure to begin a project.

Understanding these terms will help you read patterns more effectively and confidently execute projects.

Choosing the Right Cord and Supplies

Selecting the right materials is essential for both the aesthetic and functional aspects of your macramé projects. Here are some key considerations:

Cord Material:

- Cotton: Soft, durable, and easy to work with, making it ideal for beginners.
- Hemp: Strong and eco-friendly, with a natural appearance.
- Jute: Rustic and sturdy, suitable for projects that require a more rugged look.
- Nylon: Smooth and available in vibrant colors, often used for jewelry and intricate designs

Cord Thickness:

- 3-6 mm: Ideal for most projects, including wall hangings and plant hangers.
- 0.5-2 mm: Used for micro-macramé projects like jewelry

When selecting your materials, consider the look and feel you want for your project and the level of detail and durability required. With the right cords and tools, you canyou'll start your macramé journey and bring your creative visions to life.

SETTING UP YOUR WORKSPACE

Creating a dedicated workspace for your macramé projects can enhance your crafting experience. A well-organized and comfortable environment will help you focus on your creativity and produce your best work. Here's how to set up the perfect macramé workspace:

1. Choose the Right Location: Select a space in your home that is well-lit and free from distractions. Natural light is ideal, but if that's impossible, use adjustable lamps to provide ample illumination. Ensure your workspace is comfortable and has enough room to move around and work efficiently.

2. Organize Your Tools and Materials: Keeping your tools and materials organized will save time and make your crafting process more enjoyable. Here are some tips for organizing your workspace:

3. Storage Solutions: Use shelves, bins, or drawers to store your cords, beads, and other supplies. Clear containers are

helpful for quickly identifying contents. Consider a pegboard for hanging tools and keeping them within reach

4. Cord Management: Use cord spools or bobbins to keep your cords untangled and ready to use. Label cords by size and material to quickly find what you need.

5. Tool Kit: Keep a small toolkit on your workspace with essential items like scissors, measuring tape, and clips. A toolbox or caddy can help keep these items organized and portable.

Set Up a Comfortable Work Surface

Your work surface should be stable and comfortable to prevent strain during long crafting sessions. Consider these options for your work surface:

- Work Table: A sturdy table or desk provides a solid surface for large projects. Ensure the height allows you to work comfortably without hunching over
- Macramé Board: A macramé board or corkboard with T-pins can hold your work in place and provide a flat, portable surface for smaller projects.
- Vertical Workstation: Use S-hooks or a clothing rack to create a vertical workstation for projects like wall hangings. This setup allows you to stand while working, offering a different perspective and reducing fatigue.

Consider Ergonomics and Comfort

Crafting can be a prolonged activity, so ensure your workspace is ergonomically friendly to minimize discomfort:

- Seating: Choose a comfortable chair with good back support. Consider a standing desk option to alternate between sitting and standing.
- Lighting: Adjust lighting to reduce glare and eye strain. Position lights to eliminate shadows on your work surface Breaks and Stretching: Incorporate regular breaks and stretching exercises into your crafting routine to maintain physical comfort and focus.

Personalize Your Space

Finally, make your workspace inspiring and motivating. Add personal touches like artwork, plants, or music to create a space that reflects your style and encourages creativity.

With a well-organized and comfortable workspace, you'll be ready to explore the art of macramé with ease and joy. Setting up the right environment will help you focus on your projects and bring your creative visions to life.

WHY IS MACRAMÉ SO POPULAR

What is so great about macramé, anyway? So many things!

Here are three awesome things about macramé attributed to itsit's popularity over the years.

1. Mindfulness

Doing macramé is a great way to incorporate mindfulness into your daily life. And Practicing mindfulness is good for our well-being, but sometimes it's hard to squeeze 30 or even 5 minutes into your day! Once you get the hang of the basic knots, tying them becomes one of those skills that you can do without much thought.

Sitting in with a nice cup of tea and working on a section of whatever project you have on your rack is so relaxing and calming. Macrame is an excellent choice if you're looking for a hobby to bring more peace into your life.

2. Creativity

Once you know a few knots, you can use them to create patterns and shapes in your macrame. If you have a basic shape or design in mind, you can sit down and plan it out on paper to figure out the pattern. Or, you can wing it and see what beautiful piece comes out!

3. Business Potential

Want to start some creative side hustle or business? Macrame is a fabulous option!

You can make and sell original pieces on Etsy or at your local craft market, create patterns to sell online or teach others how to do macramé on your blog or YouTube channel.

If you do decide to go this route, be careful not to copy other people's designs to sell. Everyone works hard to create patterns and designs; spying on them could be better.

When you see someone's fantastic macramé creations and feel inspired to do your own, pick one part of it that you love and create a different version. Change, don't up, and don't just copy their desire.

One helpful tip I've seen, especially if you're in a design rut, is to take three or four designs you love and pick one thing from each. Then, put them together to create a new piece.

Sometimes, doing that helps spark your creativity, and you'll come up with another excellent idea you hadn't even considered!

CHAPTER 2

BASIC MACRAME KNOTS FOR BEGINNERS

Now that we've gathered our supplies let's dive into knotting!

The foundational macramé knots every beginner should learn are the lark's head knot, square knot, and double half hitch. Adding the wrapping knot and Rya knot to your skillset allows you to create beautiful macramé wall hangings even if you're starting!

Mounting Knots

In macramé, two primary mounting knots are used: the lark's head knot and the cow hitch knot (also known as the reverse lark's head knot). These knots are essential for attaching cords to your chosen base, whether a dowel rod, driftwood, wooden ring, metal hoop, or any other structure.

Lark's Head Knot

The lark's head knot is a staple in macramé projects and often the first knot you'll tie.

How to Make a Lark's Head Knot:

- Take the length of the macramé cord and fold it in half.
- Place the looped end over your dowel or base.

- With the folded side hanging down at the back and the loose ends at the front, bring the ends of the cord through the loop.
- Pull the ends tight to secure the knot.

ow Hitch Knot (Reverse Lark's Head Knot)

The cow hitch knot is similar to the lark's head knot but is tied in reverse.

- How to Make a Cow Hitch Knot:

- Fold your macramé cord in half.

- Place the looped end behind and over your dowel.

- With the folded side at the front and the ends hanging down at the back, thread the ends of the cord through the loop.

- Pull tight to complete the knot.

Square Knot

The square knot is one of the most crucial knots in macramé. It typically involves four cords: two center cords (filler cords) and two outer cords (working cords). A popular variation of this knot is the half-square knot. Tying multiple half-square knots creates a spiral effect, a common design in macramé projects.

How to Make a Square Knot

- Cross the left working cord over the two center cords and place it behind the right working cord.

- Bring the right working cord behind the two center cords and through the loop created by the left working cord. Pull to tighten.

- Reverse the process: bring the right working cord over the two center cords and behind the left working cord.

- Pull the left working cord behind the two center cords and through the loop created by the right working cord. Tighten to complete the knot.

Step 1

Step 2

Pull the ends to tighten

Step 3

Step 4

Pull the ends to tighten. Done!

Note

If you continue tying square knots one after the other, you'll create a square knot sennit, a series of knots forming a textured pattern often used in macramé projects.

When making a square knot sennit, it's important to remember that the middle strings (or filler cords) don't need to be as long as the outer working cords. A helpful rule of thumb is to make the outer cords 5 to 6 times longer than the filler cords to ensure you have enough length for multiple knots.

By mastering the square knot sennit, you canyou'll add intricate detail and structure to your macramé designs, opening up endless possibilities for creativity in your projects!

Double Half Hitch Knot

The double half hitch knot, also known as the clove knot, is versatile and common in macramé. This knot allows you to create straight rows, diamond-shaped motifs, and other intricate designs.

Many beginners find the double half-hitch knot challenging, so don't worry if you don't master it immediately. The technique is straightforward; it just takes some practice to get comfortable with it.

The following instructions show how to tie a horizontal double half-hitch knot moving to the right. In this example, the left cord will serve as the filler cord, while the right strand will act as the working cord.

How to Make a Double Half Hitch Knot

- Form the Shape: Cross the left cord over the right cord to form the shape of a number 4.
- Create a Loop: Bring the end of the right cord up in front of the left cord, loop it over, and bring it down to form a loop.
- Repeat the Loop: Repeat step 2 similarly, moving to the right.

- **Tighten the Knot:** Pull the end of the working cord to tighten the knot. You have now completed one double-half hitch knot.
- **Continue Knotting:** If additional cords are needed, repeat steps 1-4 with the remaining cords.

With practice, the double half hitch knot will become an essential tool in your macramé repertoire, enabling you to add beautiful patterns and textures to your projects.

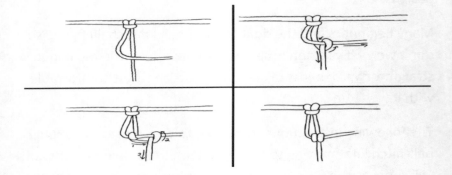

DIY Macrame Bag with Comfy Braided Handles

DIY Macramé Bag

In this chapter, I'll guide you through creating an adorable DIY macramé bag! My aim with this design was to ensure that the straps were as comfortable as possible, making the bag both functional and stylish.

To test the comfort, I filled the bag with lemons and limes and took it for a stroll with my kids—while occasionally carrying my toddler! While it might seem unusual to have a bag full of citrus fruits around the neighborhood, the experiment was a success, and the straps didn't hurt my shoulder at all.

This project is perfect for beginners who have mastered the basic knots. The macramé techniques used in this bag include:

- The square knot.
- The gathering knot.
- A four-strand braid.
- Some overhand knots at the bottom.

Supplies You'll Need to Make This DIY Macramé Bag:

- 32 strands of 3mm single-strand macramé cord, each 8 feet long, divided into 2 groups of 16
- 4 pieces of the same cord, each roughly 10 to 12 inches long (great for using scrap cord)
- Craft glue
- Masking tape

Step 1: Braid the Handles

First, we need to mark where the handles will be. For my bag, I made the braided sections approximately 22 inches long. To determine where to start braiding, I looped each group of 16 strands over a dowel and lined up the ends. This method could have been more scientific, but it worked!

Then, I measured 11 inches down from where the rope was hanging from the dowel and placed a piece of masking tape on one side. This marked the starting point for the braid, ensuring consistency and symmetry for both handles.

After marking the starting point with the masking tape, I took the taped bundle of cords off the dowel and flipped it around. Then, I secured the cords back onto the dowel using a loose knot. This setup allows you to braid the handles comfortably while keeping the cords organized and in place.

Next, I divided the cords into four groups of four strands each. Starting at the point where the tape was placed, I began a four-strand braid. As I braided, I periodically checked to ensure the braid was long enough to form a comfortable handle.

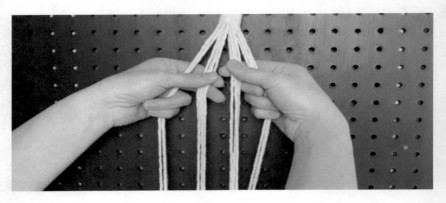

The four-strand braid is surprisingly simple once you get the hang of it. There are three basic steps to follow: crossing the right two sections, crossing the left two sections, and then crossing the middle two sections.

1. Right Section: Start with the two rightmost sections. Cross the right section over the left section.

2. Left Section: Move to the two leftmost sections. Cross the right section over the left section.

3. Middle Section: Finally, cross the left section over the right section in the middle.

Repeat this sequence until the braid reaches your desired length. This method creates a sturdy and visually appealing braid, perfect for the handles of your macramé bag.

After completing the initial braid, I taped the end to secure it. Then, I flipped the entire bundle around, removed the tape from the other side, and added a bit more braid to ensure it was even. This step helps guarantee that your handle is the correct length and centered, with equal amounts of rope hanging down on either side.

Once you're satisfied with the first handle, repeat the entire process for the second handle. After completing both, double-check to ensure they're the same length and evenly balanced.

Step 2: Tie Gathering Knots to Secure the Braids

Once you have the braided handles the way you want them, it's time to secure each end with a gathering knot. This will hold the braids in place and give your bag a neat finish.

To do this, you'll need the 4 shorter pieces of cord you prepared earlier.

How to Tie a Gathering Knot:

1. Position the Cord: Place one of the shorter pieces of cord parallel to the braid, with a small tail pointing downward.

2. Create a Loop: Form a loop with the longer end of the short cord, laying it over the braid.

3. Wrap the Cord: Wrap the long end of the short cord tightly around both the braid and the loop several times. Make sure to keep the wraps neat and close together.

4. Secure the Knot: Pass the end of the wrapping cord through the loop you created at the start.

5. Tighten the Knot: Pull on the tail of the cord that is pointing downward to tighten the loop and secure the gathering knot. Trim any excess cord if needed.

Repeat this process for both ends of each braided section, tying four gathering knots in total. This step ensures that your handles are securely fastened and ready for use.

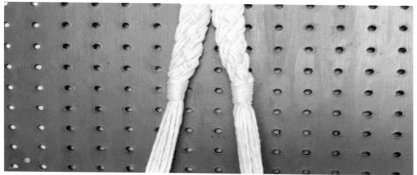

Step 3: Alternating Square Knots

The rest of the bag is crafted using alternating square knots. To ensure a consistent and even pattern, leave about an inch to an inch and a half of space between the rows.

Setup:

1. Position the Handles: Drape both handles over the dowel so that the sections you'll be working on are facing you. This allows for easier access and alignment while tying the knots.

2. Attach and Knot: Start working on the section under one of the gathering knots.

Instructions:

1. First Row: Starting on the left, skip the first two strands and make three square knots from left to right.

2. Second Row: Leave about an inch of space below the first row of knots, and then make a row of four square knots.

3. Third Row: Leave another inch of space and complete a row with three square knots.

After completing these rows on one side, flip the bag around and repeat the process on the other side, ensuring both sides are symmetrical and evenly spaced.

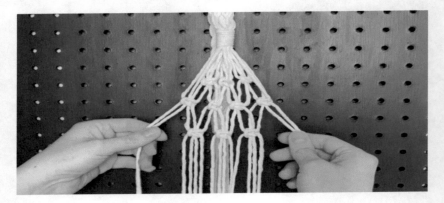

4: Connect the Centers

To bring the left and right sides of your bag together, you'll need to connect them with a square knot in the center. This step helps to create a unified, cohesive structure.

Instructions:

1. Align the Sides: Line up the left and right sides of the bag, ensuring everything is straight and even. This will help maintain the bag's symmetry and overall appearance.

2. Tie the Connecting Square Knot: Find the center strands of the bag and tie a square knot, connecting the left and right sides. Make sure this knot is even with the third row of square knots you made previously.

This connecting knot will secure the two halves of your bag and add strength and stability to the overall design.

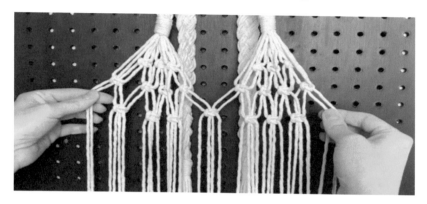

Once you've tied the connecting square knot in the center, you'll now have a row of square knots running across this side of the bag.

3. Add another Row: Make one more row of alternating square knots about an inch or so below the current row. This will add structure and texture to your bag.

Step 5: Repeat on the Other Side

Flip the bag around and repeat all the steps you did on the first side for the second side. Ensure that the rows of knots are aligned with the first side so everything lines up properly. This ensures symmetry and balance in your bag's design.

Step 6: Attach the Sides

Now it's time to attach the sides of the bag together to create the final structure.

1. Tie Side Knots: Use the two cords hanging on the left side of the front and back parts of the bag. Tie a square knot that is even with the third row of square knots from the top. This will connect the sides securely and help the bag maintain its shape.

Fill in the blanks by going down one row and tying a square knot in the places to the bottom left and right of the first connecting square knot.

The fourth row of knots will be even with these knots.

Repeat the procedure on the other side of the bag. At this point, you need to resemble a tube with handles.

Continue constructing rows of alternating square knots to complete the bag's body.

I made ten rows total, but you might extend it if you want.

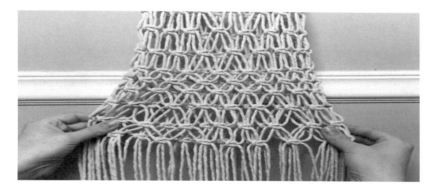

For visual interest, you may make a few rows in the center of the bag a bit closer together, as I did.

You may also choose to keep them all evenly spaced apart. If you leave more room between the knots, it will move more quickly.

Step 8: Tie the Bottom Together

to complete your macramé bag, you'll need to tie the bottom securely. While I tried a couple of other methods, this was the most straightforward technique I found, and the easier, the better!

I tried a few other approaches, but this was the clearest one I could find—and in my opinion, the simpler, the better!

There's one essential thing you should remember.

- Remove your bag from the dowel and hang it in the other way before you knot the bottom together.
- The orientation of the dowel's handles is seen in the image below.

It won't lie properly if you leave it hanging like this after finishing the bottom.

Instead of using a dowel, you'll need to hang it from something, like this following photo, with the handles pointing the other direction.

All of the square knots on the front and back of the bag must be lined correctly in order to tie the bottom.

Next, take the two left cords from the front and rear square knots, beginning from the far left, and tie them together as you would a shoelace.

Tie it the same way again, making a double knot. Tighten it up tightly. Using the two right cords from the front and rear square knots, repeat the process.

This should be done all the way to the bag's bottom. (For every pair of square knots, you will have two double knots.)

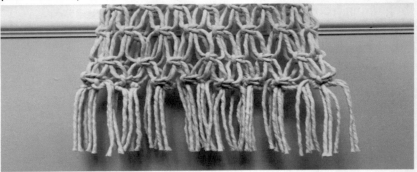

Step 9: Trim any extra rope and apply adhesive.

Trim the extra rope so that just a quarter of an inch remains protruding.

Smooth the ends against the knot after adding a little amount of glue (I used nontoxic Tacky Glue) to each knot.

After letting the glue dry, turn your bag so that the knots are now on the inside. Completed!

At this poin your bag is ready !!!

Macrame Hat Hanger Pattern

Materials Required

- 5 mm cotton macrame string, single strand
- Six 120-inch-long pieces
- A 2-inch wooden ring
- 1" wooden bead with a big hole
- Razor-sharp scissors
- Pet slicker comb or brush
- Spray for stiffening (optional)

Step First, fasten the ropes to the ring.

Using lark's head knots, secure your six pieces of rope to the wooden ring.

Next, you can hang the ring from your macrame rack or from a all nail. All you have to do is put it somewhere safe while you work.

Step 2: Create the initial diamond shape's top. Right over left, cross both centre cables.

The suitable cable that you crossed over will be the filler chord for a series of six diagonal double half hits.

To make a row of five diagonal double half hitch knots that run down and to the right, use the sixth cord from the right as the filler cord.

Flip the whole thing around to the back.

Tie five diagonal double half hitch knots in a row, traveling down and to the left, using the right center cord as the filler cord. You will not use the last cable.

Take the sixth cord from the right and make a row of four diagonal double half hitch knots moving down and to the right using it as the filler cord. The last cable on this side will also be skipped.

Flip the whole thing back around to the other side.

To make a row of four double half hitch knots that travel down and to the left, use the right center cord as the filler cord. Then, tying three double half hitch knots down and to the right, use the sixth rope from the right as the filler cord.

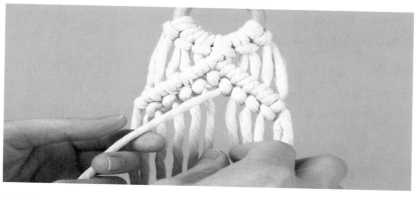

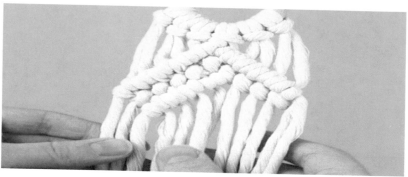

Step 3: Attach the bead.

The wooden bead will now be threaded onto the two centre wires.

I used a little piece of thin braided rope as a threader to make this step simpler.

Use the threader cord ends to thread the bead through and loop it around the two centre cords. Then, use that to draw it onto the two centre cables. This may avoid tearing the ends of   your   working   cables.

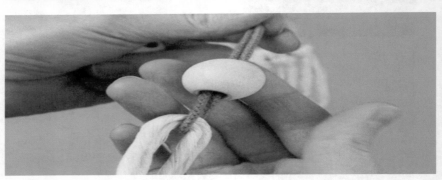

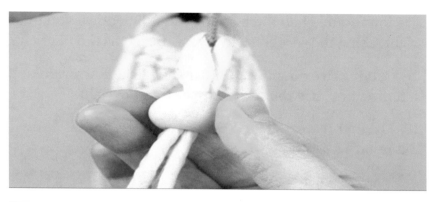

Now, to create the bottom half of the diamond, push the bead up until it touches the last row of double half-hitch knots we formed.

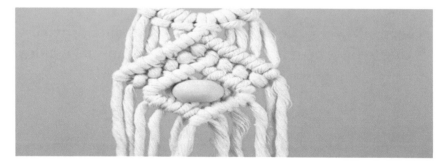

Turn everything around to the back once again.

Tie four double half hitch knots, extending down and to the right, using the second string from the left as the filler cord.

Next, tying five double half hitch knots in a downward and left direction, use the second rope from the right.

It's OK that there will be a little space between this diamond's left and right sides.

Turn everything over one again.

Tend five diagonal double half hitch knots moving down and to the right, using the far left cord as the filler cord.

Then, tying six double half hitch knots down and to the left, use the far left strand as the filler cord.

There will be a space on each side of the diamond; avoid trying to fill it in or it will get puckered. Simply let it alone.

That completes the form of the top diamond. On to the straps now!

5. Create the straps.

Divide the cables so that six are on the left and six are on the right.

Tie two square knots layered on top of one another, starting on the side you choose (I went with the left). The four inside cables will serve as fillers, while the two outside cords will serve as the working cords.

Do the same on the other side.

To create the straps, we will now tie a sequence of switch square knots.

Take the two inside cords and bring them to the outside to make a switch knot. Next, wrap the square knot around the remaining cables using those cords.

Continue doing that until you have five switch knots, spaced around two inches apart. Next, repeat the process with the other strap.

Tie a final square knot just underneath the last switch knot, just as you did at the start. Apply it on both sides.

Bring the inner two cords to the outside

use those cords to tie the square knot that makes it a "switch" knot

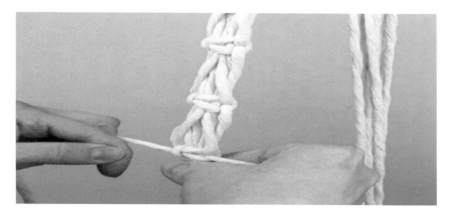

tie 5 switch knots all together

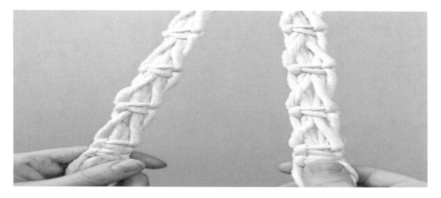

Tie one last regular square knot under the last switch knot repeat on the other side

Step 6: Make the bottom diamond shape

We will now join the two sides to form the bottom diamond.

To make a row of six double half hitch knots that travel down and to the right, use the far right cord from the left strap as the filler cord.

Next, use the sixth rope from the left as filler, tie five double half hitch knots in a downward and leftward direction.

Turn everything over one again.

Making use of the sixth chord from the right as a filler cord, make four double half hitch knots in a downward and rightward direction.

Next, make three double half hitch knots going down and to the left using the sixth rope from the left as the filler cord.

We are now going to create a square knot with the four cords in the middle.

It looks the same from both sides, so you don't have to turn it over for that portion if you don't want to. I rotated my around to the front again before I knotted the square knot.

Should you have flipped it, please turn it back immediately as we will be tying the next row of double half hitch knots in the back. You should be OK if you didn't flip it!

Tie three rows of double half hitch knots, descending and to the left, using the third rope from the right.

Turn it one final time to face the front.

Tie five double half hitch knots, traveling left and down, using the rightmost rope as the filler.

After that, tie six double half hitch knots in a downward and rightward direction using the leftmost rope as the filler cord.

Okay, the knotting is finished! Let's address the fringe now.

Step 7: Cut and tidy the fringe

You can use to make it super even, but I simply eyeballed it when I cut the fringe.

Then, if you'd like, brush yours out right now. Once brushed, give it another trim.

It is a good idea to apply hairspray or stiffening spray to prevent curling. Though I haven't done so yet, I most likely will in the near future.

slice the fringe diagonally.

Done!

Boho Macrame Wall Hanging with Tassels

Supplies You'll Need

- 12" Wooden Dowel:
- Diameter: 1/2"
- 8 mm Single Strand Cotton String:
- 6 pieces: 105" long
- 10 pieces: 22" long

Note: You might be able to cut 22" sections from two of the longest working cords after completing the diamonds. I did this, so initially, just cut 8 pieces and see if you can do the same to save some cord.

- 5 mm Single Strand Cotton String:
- 21 pieces: 8" long

Note: This cord is for the tassels, so feel free to use a different diameter if needed. If using a smaller cord, you might need a few more pieces per tassel, and if it's larger, you might need fewer pieces.

- Metal Comb
- Sharp Scissors

Instructions

Step 1: Fasten the primary cables.

Join your six 105-inch lengths of cord to the wooden dowel using lark's head knots.

Arrange them such that three are to the left and three are to the right.

Grasp the two center cords beginning on the left side of the dowel, then cross the right across the left.

Hold the cord in your right hand as the primary working cord and the cable in your left as the filler cord.

Make three double half hitch knots in a downward and leftward direction.

To make two double half hitch knots that go down and to the right, use the third rope from the right as the filler cord.

Use the far left cord as the filler cord and tie two double half hitch knots going down and to the right.

Tie three double half hitch knots moving left and down, using the far right cord as the filler cord.

The last knot will connect the bottom of the diamond.

Note:

To achieve a tilted diamond shape, angle the filler cord going down and to the Left at a lower angle than the filler cords going down and to the Right.

Step 3: Making the Other Two Diamonds on the Left

1. Start with the Left Side:

  Use the third cord from the Left as the filler cord to tie two double half hitch knots going down and to the Left.

2. Move to the Right Side:

Use the third cord from the Right as the filler cord to tie two double half hitch knots going down and to the Right.

3. Continue on the Left:

Use the far left cord as the filler cord to tie two double half hitch knots going down and to the Right.

4. Finish on the Right:

Use the far right cord as the filler cord to tie three double half hitch knots going down and to the Left.

5. Complete the Diamond:

The last knot will connect the diamond, bringing the pattern together.

To achieve three diamonds total on the left side, repeat that procedure one more time.

Step 4: On the right side, repeat the diamond design in reverse.

You will follow the same stages as for the left side diamond design, but they will be mirrored on the right side.

To start, take hold of the two middle cords and make a left-to-right crossing.

Utilize the cable in your left hand as the primary working cord and the cord in your right hand as a filler cord.

Knot three double half hitch knots in a downward and rightward direction.

Tie two double half hitch knots, one going down and one to the left, using the third string from the left as the filler cord.

Use the far right cord as the filler cord and tie two double half hitch knots going down and to the left.

Make three double half hitch knots moving down and to the right, using the far left rope as the filler cord.

Note:

This time, you'll want to make the diamonds tilt toward the left. To achieve this, angle the filler cord going down and to the right at a lower angle than the filler cords going down and to the left.

Step 5: Tie the Remaining Diamonds on the Right Side

- Start on the Right Side:
- Use the third cord from the right (the filler cord you were using) to tie two double half hitch knots going down and to the right.

Switch to the Left:

- Use the third cord from the left as the filler cord to tie two double half hitch knots going down and to the left.

Continue on the Right:

- Use the far right cord as the filler cord to tie two double half hitch knots going down and to the left.

Finish on the Left:

- Use the far left cord as the filler cord to tie three double half hitch knots going down and to the right.

Complete the Diamond:

- The last knot will connect the bottom of the diamond.
- Repeat the Process:

- Repeat the above steps to create a total of three diamonds on the right side.

Step 6: Connecting the Two Sides

To connect the two sides, follow these steps:

- Gather the Center Cords:
- Grab the two right cords from the left side and the two left cords from the right side (the centre 4 cords).

Tie a Square Knot:

- Use these centre 4 cords to tie a square knot, effectively joining the two sides and forming a continuous pattern across your macramé piece.

Next, take the two center cords, cross them over to the left and right, and tie three double half hitch knots, down and to the right, using the cord in your right hand as the filler cord.

Tie two double half hitch knots, one going down and one to the left, using the sixth rope from the left as the filler cord.

Tie two double half hitch knots moving down and to the left, using the fourth rope from the right as the filler cord.

Tie three double half hitch knots, one at the top and one at the bottom, using the fourth rope from the left as the filler cord.

The diamond will be connected with the final knot.

Step 7: Adding fringe

Check to determine whether the two longest cords dangling at the bottom have an additional 22 inches of length that may be used for fringe pieces before we add the fringe.

I measured from the bottom of the shortest piece of cord to the ends of the two longest pieces to make sure it was the right length for my fringe. I used it for two of my fringe pieces after cutting off the excess 22 inches.

You will want eight more pieces of fringe, totaling ten, measuring 22 inches.

Using a larks head knot, secure one piece of fringe to the upper left loop on the left side.

Then attach two pieces of fringe to the next loop down on the left, and again on the loop beneath that.

These are the loops that the outside cords between the diamonds on the leftmost edge have made.

With the same setup, repeat it on the right side.

Step 8: Tassel creation

Grasp three of the eight-inch-long rope segments.

Arrange the ends so that they pass through one of the diamonds' right central holes.

Next, pass the left ends through the diamond's left center hole.

Even the ends up, and push the ends back through to the front in the bottom of the center hole.

Tighten the Rya knot by pulling the ends to make everything even.

With every diamond, repeat that.

Step 9: Finishing up

Brush out your tassels with your macrame comb.

Trim them up however long you want. I went with two inches for each tassel and I used my tape measure to make sure they were all even.

To make your outside fringe even, trim it. Using my tape measure once again, I decided on an 8-inch long fringe, making sure it was all the same length.

You may now choose to keep the fringe in its current state or brush it out if desired.

After brushing out the fringe's ends, I made the decision to separate the strands somewhat but not completely.

You may adjust the fringe's length to your preference.

Step 10: A hanging loop is added.

The constrictor knot is my preferred method for incorporating a hanging rope into macrame wall hangings.

Done!

This is a DIY macrame wall hanging design that I hope you liked It's an enjoyable approach to infuse your living area with bohemian flair.

Dollar Tree DIY Mini Macrame Wall Hangings

Supplies You Need

- **Dollar Store Frames:**

  - The frames used are approximately 6.5 inches on the outside and about 5.5 inches on the inside. Feel free to use different sizes as long as they are similar.

  - **Note:** If your frame comes with glass, be sure to remove it.

- **Wooden Dowel:**

  - A 3/16 inch dowel, 12 inches long, is recommended. You can cut this dowel to fit the inside width of your frame for both pieces of wall art. Measure the inner width of your frame and cut the dowel accordingly.

- **Cardstock:**

    - Cut two pieces of cardstock to cover the image on the backing board of the wall art. If your frame has a removable image, you can skip this step.

- **3 mm Single Strand Macramé Cord:**

    - **Wall Hanging 1:** 10 pieces, each 22 inches long

    - **Wall Hanging 2:** 7 pieces, each 30 inches long, and 5 pieces, each 20 inches long

        - **Note:** If you desire longer fringe, add about 5 or 6 inches to each cord length.

- **Comb or Brush for Fringe:**

    - Used to brush out the fringe for a finished look.

- **Hot Glue Gun with Glue Sticks:**

    - Essential for securing the macramé to the dowel and attaching components to the frame.

Step 1: Tying the knots

Using lark's head knots, first fasten the ten pieces of cord to your tiny dowel. Once they are all fastened, all you need to do is secure your dowel to your work area with some Scotch tape.

We will now tie many square knots.

Take the four strands and make a square knot starting from the far left. After that, continue doing so across until you have five knots in total.

The following row will include skipping the first two cords on the left and using the remaining four cords to create a square knot. After that, you'll repeat it across to get four square knots in total. The last two chords are similarly skipped.

You will skip the first four cords for the third row, tie three square knots, then skip the last four cords for the second-to-last row.

Continue in this manner until the square knots form an upside-down triangle. One square knot will be positioned in the middle of the last row.

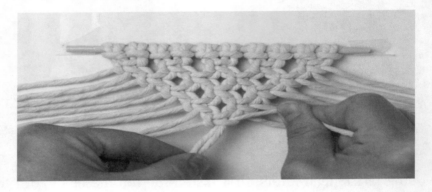

Step 2: Trimming the fringe

It's time to trim the fringe now.

I simply placed my frame on top and used some Scotch tape to indicate the approximate location of where I wanted the fringe to be cut.

Then, while I was cutting the fringe, I held my wall upright. Cuts much more straight when you use the tape as a guide.

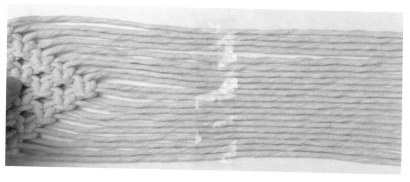

Once the fringe has been clipped, apply a little layer of hot glue on the back of the dowel and secure it firmly inside the frame.

First wall hanging complete!

Second Small Macrame Wall Hanging

The second wall hanging will be a macrame semicircle that we make.

Row 1: Use lark's head knots to secure two of the 30-inch sections to the dowel, then tape your work to the surface.

Utilizing the left cord as a filler, tie three double half hitch knots crossing to the right with it.

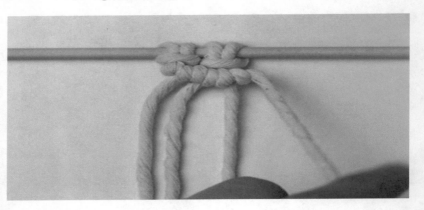

We're going to use a one-sided lark's head knot to secure our cord to this dowel after you've completed your three double half hitch knots.

You must untape this side in order to reach behind the dowel, so bring your cord in front of and above the dowel.

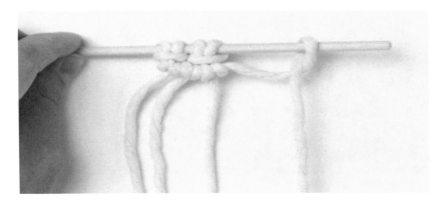

Subsequently, lower the end behind you, thread it through the loop you just created, and tighten it up beside the other knots.

It will now be raised behind the dowel, lowered in front of it, and then lowered through the loop once again.

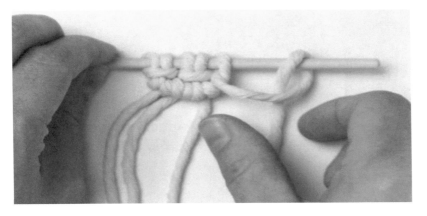

Row 2: Tie a lark's head knot on a second, thirty-inch length of rope to the right of the first two knots.

Next, you'll reattach your dowel and tie four double half hitch knots crossing to the left using the rightmost cord as your filler.

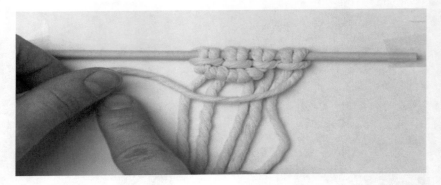

There will be a large area after you have completed the fourth one. We now have to supplement our filler cable with another cord.

Using a reverse Lark's head knot called a cow hitch, secure one of the 20-inch cables to the filler cord.

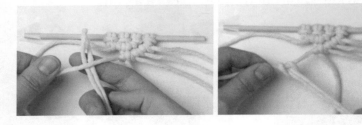

Complete your last double half hitch knot of the row by sliding it up next to the previous one so it blends in.

After that, you should bring this end of the rope up in front of the dowel.

After lowering the end through the loop, you will raise it behind the dowel and lower it through the loop once again.

Rows 3–6

This procedure will be repeated for each row.

Repeat again at the beginning of the row with your next 30-inch length of cord attached over and your dowel taped back in place. Proceed in the same manner, making double half hitch knots across until you get to a gap. After that, add a further 20 inches of rope.

When you get to a space in each row, you will add one 20-inch cable.

At the conclusion of each row, fasten your filler string to the dowel using a one-sided lark's head knot.

It will take six rows to complete.

severing the fringe

When you've completed six rows, it's time to trim the fringe. I basically eyeballed it, using the shortest piece of fringe as a reference. If you would want it to be more accurate, you may measure.

Give your fringe another cut and brush it out if you'd like.

It's time to attach the adhesive now. Carefully attach the dowel in place by applying a little layer of hot glue on its back.

Done!

WALL HANGING) PLANT HANGER

Supplies You'll Need

- The following lengths of twisted 3-ply macrame rope measuring 3 mm
- Ten cords measuring 134 inches long—roughly two arm widths, if you choose to measure that way—
- One 50-inch-long string (for the wrapping knot)
- 8-inch wooden dowel (I used a 3/4-inch dowel)
- Adorable potted plant (my container is 5.5 inches tall and 5 inches in diameter).
- savage scissors

Step 1: fasten your cables onto the dowel.

Take one of your 134" cords, fold it in half, and use a lark's head knot to fasten it to the dowel. Spread out the remaining 134" cables equally and repeat the process with them.

Use S hooks to fasten your dowel to a clothes rack, or knot a piece of cord to both ends and hang it from a doorknob or wall nail.

Step 2: Left side of the diamond in the vertical lark's head knot design

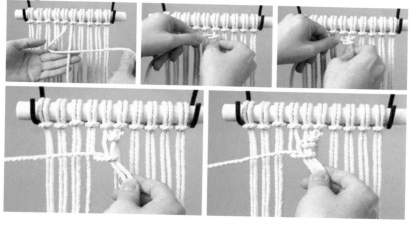

These step-by-step photographs demonstrate how to knot the diamond pattern's left top section.

Seize both centre cables. To form a half-hitch knot around the right cord, cross the left cord over the right in the manner shown in Figure 4. Then, wrap the end around and through the loop.

Tie a half hitch knot with the leftmost cord around the rightmost cord by dropping the right chord, picking up the next cord to the left, and repeating the procedure once more.

Using the leftmost cable, make a half-hitch knot around the two cords while holding them together. Then, grasp the next cord to the left.

Tie another half-hitch knot around the three cords while holding all three together and grabbing the next rope to the left.

The same cord that you used for the last half hitch knot will now be utilized.

This time, you're going to bring it behind the bundle and wrap it around the other way to the front instead of crossing it in front of the bundle in the form of a four.

Images demonstrating how to begin tying the diamond
pattern's bottom left corner.

While it is still a half hitch knot, it is now the opposite of
what we did before.

That is what you will do, returning each cable to the center.
One half of the diamond will then be finished.

The diamond's right side

We will now carry out the whole procedure again on the right
side.

Therefore, take hold of the two cords that are closest to the
center. Then, wrap the rightmost cord around the leftmost

chord in front of the cord, forming a four, similar to the first half of the left side, and bring the end through the loop.

Repetition begins when you hold the two cables together and grasp the next cord to the right. Continue in that manner until you get to the last chord on the right.

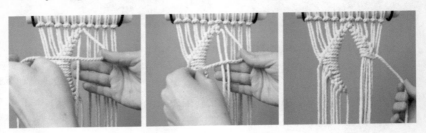

Images demonstrating how to begin tying the diamond pattern's right upper side.

Now, make a 4-pointed hold of the same rope that you used for the last knot, wrap it around, and pull it through the loop.

Just like we did on the left side, but in the other direction, repeat that for each chord returning to the center.

Connect the Diamond

To join the two sides, take the right center cord, wrap it in a figure of four around the left center cord, and tie a half hitch knot.

 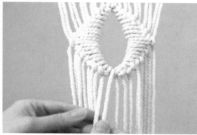

Images demonstrating how to join the diamond pattern's bottom.

Repetition

We'll move on to the plant pot holding portion when you've completed two more identical repetitions of the diamond pattern.

Step 3: To hold the plant container, tie square knots.

About 5 inches should be dropped from the final diamond. Four square knots will be tied in a row, straight across.

Tie four square knots, skipping the first two cords, and then skip the last two cords.

After flipping the two cords you didn't use on either side toward the center, tie a square knot about an inch below the row of square knots we just made.

After flipping the two cords you didn't use on either side toward the center, tie a square knot about an inch below the row of square knots we just made.

Next, repeat the action on the right side.

Turn your plant hanger over and tie square knots at the same level as the previous two knots the whole way around. Together, there will be five square knots.

Step 4: Tie a knot.

Using your 50" length of cord, tie a wrapping knot around each and every cord under the last row of square knots.

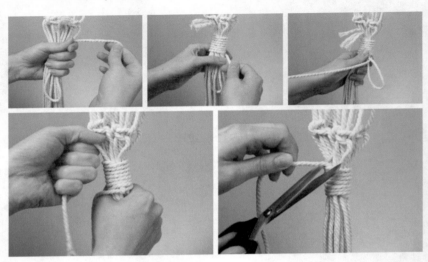

Step by step pictures that walk you through the process of tying the wrapping knot at the plant hanger's base.

Step 5: Trim the fringe to completion.

Determine the desired length of the fringe and trim off any extra. I built mine around five inches long.

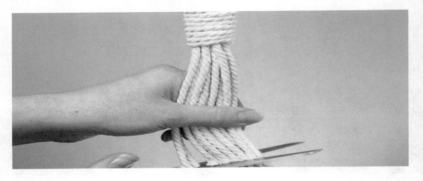

You may then choose to unravel the ends of the rope or leave them in their current state. You have the final say!

Done!

CRESCENT MOON DIY MACRAMÉ DREAM CATCHER

What You'll Need to Make a DIY Macrame Dream Catcher with Feathers: Crescent Moon

- Crescent Moon Frame, 12″ long
- Black, 3 mm twisted cotton rope (cutting instructions below)
- Pet brush with wire bristles
- Spray stiffening
- hot-glue gun
- flimsy adhesive
- savage scissors

step 1 First, fasten the ropes to the frame.

With the interior of the moon facing up, hang the crescent moon form sideways.

Nine pieces of 45-inch rope will be attached initially. After that, you'll slide them to the left and connect seven pieces of 63-inch rope to the right.

Make sure you knot a cow hitch before you join the ropes. (It's the head of a lark, but turned the opposite way.)

Next, create a half hitch on the right side by pulling the right string through the loop and up and around the frame. Apply it to the left chord as well. When it's finished, it will look like this.

See the first segment of the video if it still doesn't make sense to you. It's difficult to put into words.

This is how it will seem after all of the ropes are joined.

Step 2: Attach and tie the knots within the frame

Start by grabbing the first rope from the left and tightening it with a double half hitch knot around the frame.

Next, using the rope you just fastened to the frame and the other three cords, create a square knot.

On the left side, do the same.

Now use double half hitch knots to connect the two cords on the left to the frame.

Tie a row of square knots alternating from the first row, skipping the cords you just tied to the frame.

Tie alternate square knots for the subsequent row, skipping two more cords at the start and finish of the row. Until there are no more square knots in your row, keep going through that procedure.

It will appear as seen in the photo below on your second to last row.

Make sure all of the cables are dangling beneath the frame by pulling them through. Double half hitch knots should be used to secure each cable to the frame. To equally stretch the square knot mesh on the frame, pull the knots firmly.

Attach two on the left, then two on the right, in that order. To maintain balanced stress, go back and forth in this manner for every set.

At this point, you may cut the 45-inch cords short and save the extra for feather fringe (you'll need 8-inch pieces).

Keep the longer cables on the right in their current position.

Step 3: Continue attaching long threads to the macrame dream catcher's bottom.

The dream catcher will hang this way when it is finished, so turn it so that the long strands are hanging down at the bottom on your workbench.

14 of the 63 ropes should be tied to the bottom of the dream catcher using lark's head knots. Every knot I made had two ropes between them.

Step Four: Knot a few square knots.

Tie a square knot in the middle of the four cords that are dangling off the bottom.

Next, tie three square knots to the left and three to the right of the center, respectively.

Continue tying square knots in six more rows, skipping the two additional cords at the start and finish of each row. This is how it will seem after you're done.

Step 5: Attach the additional fringe row.

From the outside, grasp the third and fourth cords on both sides. Draw them toward the middle, then knot them in a square knot just behind the one you made before.

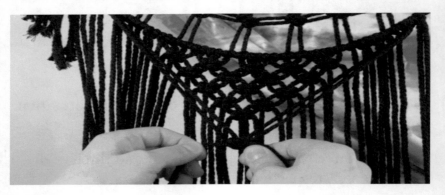

Now tie 14 lengths of 63-inch rope to the left and 14 to the right of the knot.

Double half hitch knots should be tied in a row along the fringe's left side, followed by a row on the right.

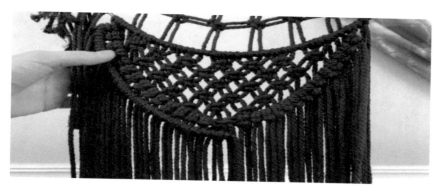

Tie a final double half hitch knot in the center to secure it.

Step 6: Create the plumes

Twenty 8-inch pieces are required for each feather.

Seize the two fringe strands in the middle. The feather fringe pieces will be attached a few inches below the double half hitch knot row.

One feather fringe piece should be folded in half and held in front of the two strands with the loop pointing to the left in order to connect it.

Next, take another piece, fold it in half, and position the loop facing just behind the two strands.

Tighten the fringe around the central cords by putting the ends of each piece through the loop of the other piece.

For the following two parts, repeat same procedure in reverse. Thus, the loops on the top piece and the bottom piece will be facing respectively to the left and right.

Ten times over, repeat the technique back and forth. To secure the fringe, make an overhand knot at the bottom.

Using the 13th and 14th strands from the exterior as the center cords, create two additional feathers, one on the left and one on the right of the macrame dream catcher. These feathers will rise over the main feather by a few inches.

It's time to buff them out and cut them into form after you've completed them all. It takes a while, but this step is sort of fun—at least I think so!

Use your pet brush to give the fringe a thorough brushing. After that, give them a double coat of stiffening spray. That's an optional step, but over time it helps them rest more comfortably and resist curling up.

Make a feather form out of the fringe.

Step 7: Complete the frame and wrap it

It's time to finish the uppermost portions of the moon frame.

Initially, my intention was to leave the ends hanging a couple of inches and then add more fringe to cover any spaces. When I removed it, the moon seemed to have a mohawk.

Rather than leaving the excess fringe in place, I chose to trim the ends, adhere them to the frame using glue, and then neatly wrap the frame. This is the method I used.

First, trim the ends to a length of approximately 1/2 inch.

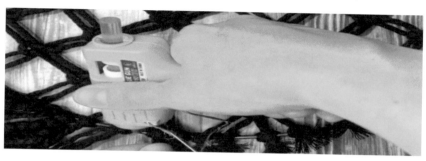

Continue doing this all the way to the edge.

I then smoothed down the ends with some sticky glue to make sure they weren't protruding everywhere in an effort to make it seem nicer.

The last 63-inch length of rope should then be wrapped around the frame. I pulled it through the little opening in the corner with a crochet hook, then wrapped it around and around all the knots.

Ensure that it completely encloses the exposed portions and ends of the frame. This is how it appears halfway through.

When you're done wrapping, secure the end of the rope in place by passing it through the last wrap. The long end simply kind of fits in with the fringe, so I left it hanging.

Restart from the beginning of the wrapping process and adhere the end to the rear of the frame using adhesive.

To add some interesting texture, you may now untwist some of the long fringe strands.

Completed!

You are welcome to add a hanger if you'd want, but I didn't. Right now, all I'm doing is hanging my macrame dream catcher on a nail.

TROUBLESHOOTING AND TIPS

Creating beautiful macramé projects involves mastering various techniques and overcoming challenges. This section will help you troubleshoot common mistakes, achieve perfect tension, and apply finishing techniques to enhance your work.

Common Mistakes and How to Avoid Them

Even experienced macramé artists encounter challenges. Here are some common mistakes and how to avoid them:

1, Uneven Knots: Knots that vary in size can disrupt the pattern.

- Solution: Consistently apply the same amount of tension to each knot. Practice with scrap cords to develop a uniform technique.

2. Twisted Cords: Cords can twist during knotting, affecting the overall look.

- Solution: Regularly untwist cords by allowing them to dangle and unwind. Keep cords taut while working to minimize twisting.

3. Incorrect Knotting: Tying knots in the wrong sequence can lead to pattern errors.

- Solution: Carefully follow instructions and diagrams. Double-check each step before proceeding to the next.

4, Frayed Cords: Repeated handling can cause cords to fray.

- Solution: Use high-quality cords and handle them gently. Trim frayed ends with sharp scissors to maintain a neat appearance

Tips for Perfect Tension

Achieving the correct tension is critical to producing professional-looking macramé pieces. Here are some tips to help you maintain consistent tension:

- Practice Consistency: Consistent tension comes with practice. Regularly check your knots to ensure they are uniform in size and appearance.
- Use a Tensioning Tool: Consider using a macramé board or corkboard with T-pins to hold cords in place, allowing you to focus on knotting without worrying about slippage
- Adjust Grip and Pressure: Experiment with different grips and pressure levels to find what works best for you. Keep your grip firm but relaxed to avoid over-tightening knots
- Work in Sections: Divide your project into sections, focusing on maintaining tension in each part before moving on. This approach helps prevent tension inconsistencies across the entire piece

Finishing Techniques

Finishing touches add polish and professionalism to your macramé projects. Here are some techniques to consider:

- Trimming and Fringing: Use sharp scissors to trim excess cord ends. For fringe, unravel the ends and comb them out for a soft, even look.
- Securing Knots: To prevent knots from unraveling, apply a small amount of fabric glue or clear nail polish to the ends of the knots for added security.
- Hemming and Binding: Hemming involves folding and sewing cord ends to prevent fraying. Binding cords with decorative wraps or thread can add a finished look and reinforce areas subject to wear.
- Blocking: Blocking involves shaping and fixing your piece in place to maintain its form. Pin your project to a board and spray it with water, allowing it to dry in the desired shape.

Conclusion

As you reach the end of this macramé journey, I hope you have discovered the joy and satisfaction that comes from creating with your own hands. Macramé is more than just an art form; it's a way to express creativity, find relaxation, and connect with a rich tradition of craftsmanship.

The Joy of Creating with Macramé

Every knot you tie, and every pattern you complete is a testament to your patience, creativity, and skill. The beauty of macramé lies in its simplicity and versatility—transforming simple cords into stunning works of art. Whether you're crafting a wall hanging, a plant holder, or a piece of jewelry, each project is an opportunity to explore your imagination and bring your unique vision to life.

Macramé is also a meditative practice, offering a chance to step away from the hustle and bustle of daily life. The rhythmic repetition of knots can be soothing, allowing you to focus and find peace in the process. As you continue to create, remember that the journey is just as important as the finished piece.

Continuing Your Macramé Journey

The world of macramé is vast and full of possibilities. As you grow more confident in your skills, I encourage you to explore new techniques, experiment with different materials, and challenge yourself with more complex projects. Here are some ways to continue your macramé journey:

- Expand Your Skills: Try incorporating advanced knots, adding beads and embellishments, or experimenting with color through dyeing.
- Join a Community: Connect with fellow macramé enthusiasts online or in local craft groups. Sharing your work and learning from others can be inspiring and motivating.
- Teach Others: Consider sharing your knowledge and passion by teaching friends or hosting workshops. Teaching can deepen your understanding and appreciation of the craft.
- Explore Other Crafts: Macramé can be combined with other crafts, such as weaving, crochet, or even sewing, to create hybrid projects that push the boundaries of traditional macramé.

As you continue your macramé journey, embrace the challenges and celebrate your successes. Each piece you create reflects your creativity and dedication.

If you enjoyed this book and found it helpful, please take a moment to leave a positive review. Your feedback not only helps me improve future editions but also encourages other aspiring macramé artists to explore this beautiful craft.

Thank you for embarking on this journey with me. I hope macramé brings you as much joy and fulfillment as it has brought to countless others throughout history.

22850349R00064